PALMERS OF JARROW

1851-1933

Jim Cuthbert and Ken Smith

Tyne Bridge Publishing

Acknowledgments:
The authors would like to thank the following for their kind help in the preparation of this book: Brian Aitken, editor, The Journal, Newcastle, for permission to use photographs from the Newcastle Chronicle & Journal library; Joan McIntyre; Margaret Harle; Christine Harle; Dick Keys; Joe Clarke; John Dobson; Ron French; the Jarrow and Hebburn Local History Society; and the staff of Newcastle and South Shields Libraries.

Cover design: A.V. Flowers

Illustrations:
Photographs are reproduced from the Local Studies Collection at Newcastle City Library unless otherwise indicated.

Front cover: A warship lies near the Jarrow-Howdon ferry landing, c.1910.
Back cover: The Jarrow Crusade, 1936 (courtesy of Newcastle Chronicle & Journal Ltd.)

©Jim Cuthbert and Ken Smith, 2004.

ISBN 1857951964

Published by
City of Newcastle upon Tyne
Education & Libraries Directorate
Newcastle Libraries & Information Service
Tyne Bridge Publishing, 2004

www.tynebridgepublishing.co.uk

Printed by Elanders Hindson, North Tyneside

The launch of HMS Lord Nelson, *September 4th 1906.*

Contents

The lot of a Palmers workman was one of hard toil and long hours. Here, a man uses a new caulking tool, early 1900s.

The pioneering steam collier John Bowes *passes the Palmers shipyard at Jarrow 54 years after her launch at the yard. The distinctive gantries of Palmers'
cableway cranes tower above the Tyne.*

Fast and Reliable

In 1851-52 businessman Charles Mark Palmer and his brother George set up a shipyard at Jarrow on the south bank of the River Tyne between Hebburn and South Shields. The new company occupied the site of an earlier yard where wooden warships had been built for the Royal Navy during the Napoleonic Wars.

But the Palmer brothers had iron steamships in mind rather than wooden sailing vessels when they founded their business in the small colliery village of Jarrow. That village, famed as the monastic home of the earliest English historian, the Venerable Bede, would grow by the early 1900s into a town of around 40,000 people.

This growth was in great measure due to the expansion of the shipyard which earned a worldwide reputation for its soundly constructed vessels. Indeed, the livelihoods of the people of Jarrow became almost entirely dependent upon the success of Palmers, a weakness which would leave its workers tragically exposed to unemployment during the Great Depression of the early 1930s.

As well as berths for the construction of vessels, Charles Palmer went on to establish blast furnaces, iron and steel works, and boiler and engine works on the site, making it a major hive of industry which by 1909 stretched nearly three quarters of a mile along the southern bank of the Tyne opposite Howdon. The company had the highest output of ships in Britain in 1877, 1879, from 1880 to 1883, and again in 1888 and 1889.

During its lifetime of over 80 years Palmers was to launch more than 900 ships. The first vessel constructed was the iron paddle tug *Northumberland*, launched in April 1852. It was a small and seemingly insignificant step for a business which would develop into an extraordinary success story for Charles, a man with major interests in coal mining as well as shipbuilding. By the early 1900s Palmers was employing between 8,000 and 10,000 men and boys when the order books were full.

It was coal from the pits of County Durham which had spurred Charles to begin his shipbuilding venture with his brother. His aim was to launch iron steam collier ships to carry coal to London on a regular basis. In those days this was a bold idea. The sea coal carrying trade at that time was totally dominated by small wooden sailing vessels.

The second ship launched was therefore a steam collier, driven by a propeller and with an iron hull. This vessel was the pioneering *John Bowes*, launched into the river on June 30, 1852. Besides Charles himself, among those almost certainly present on this occasion was the yard's first manager, John McIntyre, who was the inventor of an improved type of water ballast tank for use in ships.

A painting of John Bowes *under sail off the mouth of the Tyne.*

The founder. Charles Mark Palmer at the age of 30 at the beginning of his career as a ship-builder at Jarrow.

Charles Palmer, born at South Shields in 1822, was the son of a Tyneside shipowner and timber merchant. Receiving his earliest education in his home town, he later went to the highly regarded Dr Bruce's Academy in Percy Street, Newcastle, a school attended by the sons of the wealthy or comfortably placed inhabitants of North-East society.

In 1847 Charles joined the firm of John Bowes as a managing partner. The firm became a major coal-owner in County Durham. As well as mining, the business also began coke production and Charles was involved in this venture. It was Palmer's connections with mining which were a major factor in the foundation of the yard.

The *John Bowes*, appropriately named after the head of the coal-owning concern, was the first vessel to demonstrate conclusively the advantages of employing steam as the motive power for carrying coal on the sea. She was also the first steamship built specifically to transport 'black diamonds' from the pits of the North-East to London on a regular basis. But she was not the first steam collier; the *Bedlington*, of 1841, and the *Q.E.D.*, of 1844, both launched on the Tyne, were earlier but less commercially successful examples of this type of vessel.

However, it was the *John Bowes* which was to cause the greatest stir in the North-East.

Competition from steam on the land had prompted Charles to launch this trail-blazing ship. The development of railways had led to the fast delivery of coal from the pits of the northern Midlands and south Yorkshire to London and the South-East. There was a huge increase in the amounts transported by steam trains. The more distant mines of the North-East were at a distinct disadvantage and Charles decided to overcome this challenge by delivering coal in steamships. But steamships were still in their infancy and many doubted that such an idea was feasible.

Charles later said: 'About the year 1850 the carriage of the coal by rail began seriously to affect the sale of North Country coal on the London market, and it became essential to devise means of conveying the staple product of this district to London in an expeditious, regular, and, at the same time, economical manner.'

The *John Bowes* demonstrated that a steamship, equipped with engines, was faster and far more reliable than a sailing vessel, which was dependent on the vagaries of the wind. The new ship, capable of carrying 650 tons of cargo, was fitted with an engine supplied by the firm of Robert Stephenson, of Forth Banks, Newcastle, and she had a speed of around eight or nine knots. The vessel also featured arrangements for water ballasting, then a relatively new feature.

The *John Bowes* left the Tyne on her maiden voyage with a cargo of 500 tons of coal on July 27 1852, and halted at Sunderland for compass adjustment. From there, it took her two days to reach London, two days to discharge her cargo in the Thames and she was back in the Tyne on August 3. The round voyage had taken her only seven days, as against a sailing collier's usual month.

The ship had a long life. She lasted an extraordinary 81 years, during which she served as a stores vessel in the Crimean War, had several changes of name, survived numerous collisions and carried general cargoes as well as coal. She also received improved engines and boilers.

The launch of the iron screw steam collier John Bowes *at the Jarrow yard on June 30th 1852. This ship was an important pioneer of steam power on the coal voyages from the Tyne to London. She was built on a slipway where wooden warships had been launched during the Napoleonic Wars by the firm of Simon Temple. Palmers Yard was established on the site of Temple's yard. Coal owners and manufacturers were among the large number of people who attended the event. Guests included the Mayor and Sheriff of Newcastle. It was 2.15 in the afternoon, at high water, when the 148 foot long vessel glided into the Tyne without any major problem. The naming ceremony was performed by Charles Palmer's first wife, Jane.*

The ship's iron hull was almost certainly patched up many times, but iron hulls often lasted a good number of years. The career of the *John Bowes* ended in 1933 when, under the name *Villa Selgas*, she sank after developing a leak off the north coast of Spain. All the crew were saved.

The success of this ship led to the building of many other steam colliers at the Palmer yard. Among these were the *William Hutt* (named after another John Bowes partner), *Countess of Strathmore* (named after John Bowes' mother, but wrecked on her maiden voyage), *Northumberland*, *Sir John Easthope*, *Durham*, *Jarrow*, *Phoenix* and *Marley Hill*. All were launched in the early 1850s.

The *Jarrow* was the first ship to have an engine built at the Palmer yard. Charles was evidently particularly proud of this achievement. In November 1853 the company provided dinner at the Golden Lion Hotel at South Shields for 150 workmen to celebrate the fitting of this machinery. The *Jarrow* proved, like most of her sisters, to be a highly successful vessel. In 1854, for example, she made 29 voyages to London, delivering no less than 18,000 tons of coal.

The yard went on to build the first 'flat-iron' colliers. These were ships designed with very low superstructures, shallow draft and hinged funnels and hinged masts which could be lowered, enabling them to pass under the numerous Thames bridges. They were thus able to sail far up the river to deliver their coal to gas works and, in later years, electricity power stations deep within the London area.

The earliest 'flat-irons' were the *Roystone* (soon after renamed *Westminster*) and *Vauxhall*, both launched by Palmers in 1878. The *Vauxhall* made her 1,000th voyage to London in 1896. She averaged nearly 60 such trips a year, sailing regularly to the Nine Elms Gas Works on the Thames and generally carrying about 1,000 tons of coal on each occasion. Her long-time master, Captain A.W. Wood, was a Jarrow man, as were several members of the crew.

The steam collier William Hutt, *built by Palmers. In later years she was used as a cable ship and is seen here laying a telegraph cable between Britain and Belgium in heavy seas, 1853.*

The ship's life, plying back and forth between the Tyne and the London river, was not without its dramatic moments. She was in collision several times.

For example, in October 1888 the *Vauxhall* and the Palmer-built *Prudhoe Castle* collided in the mouth of the Tyne. The *Vauxhall* sank, but was later refloated. The other vessel did not go down, although she suffered damage.

In May 1905 the *Vauxhall* was in collision with the Palmer-built tanker *Broadmayne*, again in the mouth of the Tyne. All 17 crewmen from the collier took to the ship's boats and were landed safely at North Shields. During the next week the *Vauxhall* was refloated. The pioneering 'flat iron' had proved to be a true survivor.

She lasted almost 10 more years and then her luck ran out during the First World War, although enemy attack was not to blame. In January 1915 the *Vauxhall* struck a sunken vessel near the Sherringham Shoal off the Norfolk coast and became a total wreck. She had been on passage from Seaham to London. The vessel's long career was finally over.

Ships and Steel

Blast furnaces for the production of pig-iron were set up at the Jarrow yard in 1857 and these were soon followed by rolling mills. At about the same time, Palmers acquired the rights to mine iron ore close to the coast of North Yorkshire, between Saltburn and Whitby.

However, the area lacked a nearby suitable port from which the iron ore could be transported. Charles therefore had a harbour, known as Port Mulgrave, built close to the mines at a cost of £30,000, an enormous sum in those days, so that a fleet of company-owned ships could receive the ore safely.

These vessels sailed northwards to the Tyne, bringing their cargo to the quay alongside the blast furnaces at the western end of the yard. Higher grade hematite ore was also shipped in from Spain to produce iron and steel of better quality.

A considerable amount of the iron and steel was used to build Palmer vessels and it was said that the yard brought in iron ore at one end of the works and sent it away again at the other end in the form of finished ships. This was literally true, but iron and steel from the works was also exported to destinations throughout Britain and worldwide.

The blast furnaces at the Jarrow yard, pictured around 1910. Iron, and later steel, were produced for the ships. The metals were also supplied to markets worldwide.

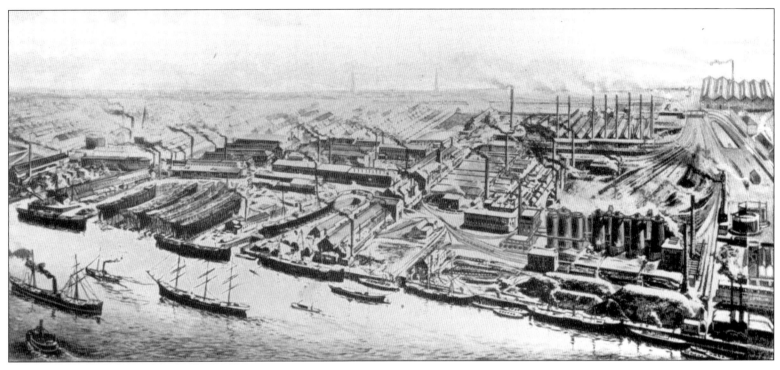

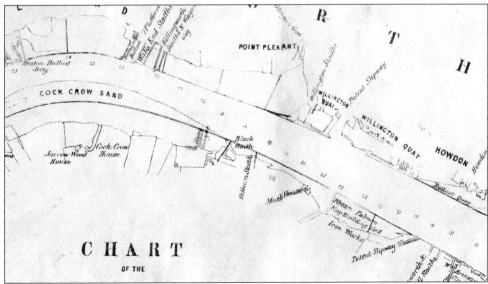

Above, Palmers c.1890 when it had expanded from the base that had been established by 1863, as shown on John Christie's pocket chart of the Tyne, left. On the chart a slipway for the repair of vessels can be seen at the east end of the yard, bottom right.

By the 1890s Jarrow had expanded from a small village to an industrial town.

The earliest Palmer ships were built of iron, but steel came into increasing use from the 1880s onwards. The first of the company's steel vessels, the *Albatross*, was launched by Miss Price, daughter of the company's general manager, John Price, in January 1884.

As we have seen, in addition to building ships, the yard began constructing the propelling machinery for them. The site's engine works supplied the machinery for the majority of vessels launched.

By the late 1880s an observer looking from the northern bank of the Tyne towards the yard would see (as he peered through the smoke) at the site's western end the iron ore quay where ships discharged the ore. Immediately behind were the blast furnaces for producing the pig-iron. Then, as the eye moved down river (eastwards) came the rolling mills, foundry and boiler erecting shop and behind them was the steel works.

Further on still was a 440ft-long graving dock (dry dock) for the repair of ships and to the rear of this was the engine works and a smiths' shop. Near these, towards the eastern end of the works, was the shipbuilding yard with its eight berths. Finally there were more workshops, two jetties and a 600ft-long slipway, also used for repair work. Railway lines ran throughout this great industrial base and these connected with the main outside lines via a crossing on Western Road.

But Jarrow was not to be the only shipbuilding site operated by the company. In 1859 Palmers took over a yard at Willington Quay, Howdon, on the northern bank of the Tyne. The first of its Howdon vessels was the *Port Mulgrave*, launched in March 1860, and this yard went on to build many more ships.

Merchant vessels were often in great demand, but the outbreak of the Crimean War in 1854 provided the company with an opportunity to break into the important market of warship building. The Admiralty placed an order for the armour-plated HMS *Terror*, a specialised battleship of great fire power. She was, in essence, a floating gun battery, designed to attack the Russian base of Kronstadt in the Baltic.

HMS Terror was, in essence, a floating gun battery, but she never fired a shot in anger. The ship was launched in 1856.

HMS *Terror* may have lacked the fine lines of later warships but she helped to establish Palmers' reputation with the Admiralty. Charles backed the novel idea of rolling the armour plates for this ship instead of forging them. It took only three months to complete the vessel and the process of rolling plates for ships was given tremendous impetus.

About 900 men were employed night and day to build the ship. The *Newcastle Daily Journal* described her as a 'monster floating battery' but then spoke of her as a 'precious babe' when describing the launch by Mrs George Palmer on April 24 1856.

HMS *Terror*'s sides sloped outwards towards the water and were composed of three protective coatings. First came an inner one of iron, then one of teak planking six inches thick, and then another layer, this time of rolled iron armour four inches thick. She was equipped with twenty six 68-pounder guns manufactured by Armstrong's of Elswick, Newcastle.

However, the *Terror* was too late to carry out the duties for which she was designed. The Crimean War had ended by the time the vessel was delivered. She never fired a shot in anger.

Many more warships were to follow the *Terror*. In 1862 the frigate HMS *Defence* was completed by the company, with an armour-plating four and a half inches thick, and from the 1870s onwards Palmers began receiving a large number of orders from the Admiralty. These ves-sels were built at both the Jarrow and Howdon yards.

In 1872 the coastal and harbour defence ships HMS *Cerberus* and HMS *Gorgon* were completed, the *Cerberus* being stationed in Melbourne, Australia. The year 1885 saw the delivery of two fast naval dispatch vessels, HMS *Surprise* and HMS *Alacrity*.

Between 1888 and 1905 Palmers completed eight cruisers of between 2,135 and 5,000 tons displacement. These included HMS *Orlando* (launched 1886), HMS *Rainbow* (launched 1891), HMS *Pegasus*, HMS *Pyramus* (both launched 1897) and HMS *Sapphire* (launched 1904). The *Orlando* and her sister *Undaunted* were among the first Royal Navy vessels to be fitted with triple expansion engines and these were also constructed at the Jarrow yard. In

The cruiser HMS Orlando. *Between 1888 and 1905 Palmers completed eight cruisers.* Orlando *was launched in 1886. Inset, an invitation card to the launch.*

1875-76 a series of 12 river gunboats were produced. These flat-bottomed vessels were broad in the beam and were appropriately named after rivers. They included the *Sabrina* and *Spey*, completed in 1875, and the *Tees*, *Esk* and *Tweed*, delivered the following year.

Among the battleships launched by Palmers were HMS *Resolution* and HMS *Revenge*, completed in 1893, and these were followed by HMS *Russell* (launched 1901), HMS *Lord Nelson* (launched 1906), HMS *Hercules* (launched 1910) and a second HMS *Resolution* (launched 1915). Palmers delivered its largest warship, the battle-cruiser HMS *Queen Mary*, in 1913.

The first *Resolution* was launched on May 28 1892, the ceremony being performed by the wife of the government's chief of naval construction, William White. Guests were then entertained to lunch, presided over by Charles Palmer.

Displacing 14,150 tons when complete, the ship was 380ft long and of 75ft beam. Her maximum speed was around 16.5 knots and her armour up to 17 and 18 inches thick in places. The vessel's hull was divided into 220 watertight compartments. *Resolution*'s main armament comprised four breech-loading 13.5-inch guns. Other weapons carried included ten 6-inch quick firing guns and she was equipped with seven torpedo tubes.

Battleships were certainly prestigious queens of the waves, but smaller warships proved to be a mainstay of the order book, partic-

The scene at the launch day of the battleship Resolution *at Jarrow on 28th May 1892. A second battleship named* Resolution *was launched by Palmers in 1915.*

ularly torpedo-boat destroyers, forerunners of the modern destroyer. From 1895 until 1910 the company was engaged on building no less than 28 of these vessels, fast ships with names such as *Janus*, *Lightning*, *Porcupine*, *Flying Fish*, *Flirt*, *Syren* and *Star*. The first craft in this long series were capable of speeds up to 27 knots, but later they were even more powerfully engined.

HMS *Viking*, delivered in 1910, was the largest and fastest of this early 'fleet' of torpedo-boat destroyers, displacing 1,000 tons and capable of 33 knots. Unusually, perhaps uniquely for the Royal Navy, she had six funnels. The vessel was driven by Palmers-built turbine engines.

But despite her impressive turn of speed and special looks, the ship's career was to have a less than glorious start. On May 16, 1910, the *Viking* was in collision with the tug *Triton* in thick fog near the Black Middens rocks at the mouth of the Tyne.

The *Viking* had left the Jarrow yard for trials in the North Sea with visibility clear, but near the entrance to the river she encountered the fog. A fret had rolled in from the sea. The vessel was reported to have sounded her horn continuously to warn other ships of her presence. It was to no avail. The *Viking* struck the *Triton* amidships. Luckily, the two vessels were locked together for a while and this enabled most of the 30 men aboard the tug to be rescued by the crew of the destroyer.

A ship under repair at the Palmers dry dock, Jarrow.

The tug *Victory*, which had been escorting the *Viking* towards the sea, picked up several other *Triton* men from the water. All had been saved. Afterwards, the *Viking* put her engines astern and backed away from the *Triton*, which then sank.

The torpedo-boat destroyer returned to Jarrow to have her damaged bow replaced and this delayed her delivery for over four months. It was early October before she managed to leave the Tyne.

The *Triton* had been carrying such a large number of men because she had been hired to take waterboard workers on a pleasure trip to Warkworth in Northumberland. Their excursion in the tug had come to an abrupt and early end, but at least no lives were lost.

The gathering for the launch of the torpedo-boat destroyer Star *in August 1896. The ceremony was performed by Mrs Cleveland, wife of Admiral Cleveland, a director of Palmers. The* Star *served mainly in home waters and also did a spell of duty at Gibraltar. She survived the First World War and went to the break-er's yard in 1919. Palmers was renowned for its torpedo-boat destroyers.*

Poverty and Disease

Poverty, overcrowding and disease were common features of life in Jarrow during the 19th and early 20th centuries, as they were in other areas of Tyneside, although Jarrow had a particularly high death rate. Large numbers of people in the town endured this poverty, particularly at times when work in the ship-yard was scarce. Indeed, the standard of living of the population closely mirrored the Palmers order book.

An observer wrote in December 1885: 'The distress of all kinds of work people in this town and district is awful to witness. The unemployed of this town are now in an immeasurably worse posi-tion than they were at this time last year … Thrifty workmen had saved money, some of them had a purse full. All that is gone. They are now face to face with destitution, and proud in their poverty they prefer starvation with their family to revealing their circum-stances out of doors. And yet the poor are good to the poor.'

Efforts were made through charitable donations and acts to relieve the plight of those suffering deprivation, particularly the children. For example, in March 1892 more than 6,000 breakfasts were provided for needy youngsters in the town, each child receiv-ing two such meals a week. Many of them sat down to their break-fasts at Lockhart's Cocoa Rooms in Ormonde Street and the Salem Baptist Chapel in Knight Street where Sunday school teachers served the meals.

A fund had been set up for this purpose and it relied entirely on contributions from residents and well-wishers. Even so, it had been reported the previous month that very little money was being donated to the Children's Breakfast Fund owing to the high unem-ployment in the town caused by a trade depression.

Other meals were also sometimes provided. In January 1893 the numbers of children receiving free dinners at various centres in Jarrow averaged about 1,000. It was hoped to reduce this number by about 50 as fathers found work.

The following month the community was visited by disease. Two patients with smallpox were taken to the isolation hospital at Primrose on the outskirts of the town. By the end of the month, one of them, Elizabeth Chatt, had died of the disease. The unfortu-nate girl was only 17.

Also during February 1893 a charitable fund provided clogs for schoolchildren whose parents could not afford footwear. For exam-ple, 50 clogs were distributed at St Bede's RC Schools and 64 at the Hill Street and Monkton schools. A Dr Whamond and a Mr V. Hopkinson made an urgent appeal for help with providing 50 more pairs as the fund had run out of money.

In March of that year, the town's medical officer of health, Dr G.W. Weir, reported that during the past year there had been 132 deaths from infectious diseases. These included 32 from whooping cough, 30 from diarrhoea (probably gastro-enteritis, 21 of these involving babies under 12 months), nine from typhoid, seven from diptheria, and 54 from influenza.

In May six more people contracted smallpox. The removal of the patients to the hospital for infectious diseases caused a good deal of morbid curiosity with crowds thronging the streets. Stanley Street had three cases, followed by Albion Street with two and Short Row with one.

Later that month there were seven further cases of smallpox, all from the Stanley Street and Albion Street area, which was situat-

Ormonde Street, Jarrow c.1904. Behind the bustling town centre streets lay areas of great poverty, particularly during times of unemployment.

ed between Monkton Road and Staple Road. Before the month was out, James Burrow, a boy aged five, had died in the isolation hospital. Two years later, in June 1895, there was to be another outbreak of smallpox in Jarrow.

As late as 1900 the borough medical officer of health reported that in the year ending March 31 1900, 203 children aged under one year and 323 under five had died. Forty of the infants under one had died of infectious diseases. There had been a severe outbreak of scarlet fever in the borough, 231 people, including adults, losing their lives to the illness. Other deaths from fever included 56 from typhoid and 12 from diptheria. Whooping cough claimed 18 lives and measles one.

From 1883 to 1885 the town had a death rate from infectious diseases well above the average compared with 50 other towns nationwide. The high prevalence of such illnesses amongst the community caused the medical officers of health great concern. Overcrowding, poor sanitation and inadequate nutrition, particularly in times of economic depression, were among the major factors identified as the cause.

However, overcrowding, poor sanitation and nutritional problems were experienced in many other areas of Tyneside and throughout Britain. It is not therefore entirely clear why the town had a particularly bad illness record. It may be that Jarrow experienced one or all of these problems to a greater extent than other communities.

It is possible that overcrowding was the most important factor. Drawn by the hope of employment at Palmers, workers flocked to the town, which grew at an alarming rate, with homes springing up rapidly, many families living in close proximity to one another in overcrowded accommodation. Workmen on their own seemed to have fared little better than families. Lodging houses were said to contain beds which always remained warm as they were occupied night and day by a succession of men working shifts.

Despite this, the issue of sanitation caused as much disquiet as

A back yard in Jarrow photographed in 1933 before slum clearance. Conditions had not greatly improved over the years and sanitation was evidently still a concern. Most of the worst housing was to the north of the railway line, nearer to the river.

overcrowding. In the early years of the developing town, many workmen and their families lacked proper sanitary arrangements, with heaps or pits known as middens, outside houses, being used for waste disposal. Closets with ash pits appear to have been provided for a considerable number of dwellings, but it is clear that sanitation was primitive by today's standards. Water from middens seeped into the ground around houses, into streets and under buildings, polluting surface water and creating ideal conditions for illnesses.

Sanitation seems to have been slow to improve, although box closet lavatories were gradually introduced. Box closets were an advance, but still far from satisfactory, and the town council was criticised for slowness in emptying them and in cleaning back streets. In 1897 a letter to the *Jarrow Express* stated that 'the box closets in nine out of 20 cases resemble sewerage exits ...' The writer added: 'So long as such a state of things as this exists we shall still be pestered with outbreaks of fever and other dreaded diseases.' He also declared: 'The back lanes in most cases in the poorer areas are strewn with all sorts of decaying vegetable and animal matter.'

Another hazard also beset the community. Smoke and grit from the blast furnaces and iron and steel works added to the unhealthy environment of the town. In 1900, for example, Jarrow Town Council decided to take legal action against Palmers to compel the

Grange Road, Jarrow, c.1900. The town suffered from a high prevalence of infectious diseases.

company to do something about the problem in Western Road. This area was showered with black smuts and grit on a daily basis. Residents and shopkeepers complained that it was difficult for people to walk along Western Road without getting something in their eyes. The footpaths were covered in lumps of black grit and this nuisance also affected other parts of the town when the wind blew from the north.

But ill health and pollution were not the only problems with which the people of Jarrow had to cope. The severe depression in the shipbuilding industry which gripped the rivers Tyne and Wear in 1893 led to reductions in wages.

In April, North-East shipbuilding labourers of the National Labour Union were informed by their delegates that the employers would be reducing their pay in a month's time. Piece rates would be cut by five per cent and there would be one shilling and sixpence off time rates of 30 shillings (£1.50) and over. In addition, time rates of 20 shillings (£1) and below 30 shillings would be reduced by one shilling and five pence. Workers in all the other shipyard trades were also having similar cuts forced upon them.

The coaly Tyne. A ferry passes the smoky chimneys of Palmers yard at Jarrow c.1900.

The following year did not seem to bring much improvement in the economic situation. A correspondent declared in the *Jarrow Guardian*: 'Not withstanding that a considerable number of workmen have recently left the Mid-Tyne area for Barrow and the Clyde and other places, the number of idle men is still on the increase, and in such a large centre of industry as Jarrow, Hebburn and Wallsend, the suffering among the labouring population is becoming daily more acute.'

Bad winter weather in early 1895 caused more men to be laid off, open-air work at the Jarrow yard being brought to a halt. A 'Poor Bairns Clog Fund' was started.

Charles Palmer and his wife made a contribution of £50 to help the children of unemployed fathers and also gave 50 tons of coal to the mayor of Jarrow for distribution to the poor. Ninety pairs of clogs were given out to the youngsters as a result of the fund.

However, by 1897 the work situation in the town had improved considerably. Palmers had the fifth highest output of shipping in Britain that year. A total of 40,319 tons was launched from the yards at Jarrow and Howdon, comprising 13 vessels. It was an increase of 4,134 tons over the previous year. C.S. Swan & Hunter at Wallsend had been the only shipbuilding company on the Tyne with a greater output.

By the early 20th century many small homes had sprung up close to the yard, north of the railway line between Newcastle and South Shields. These were often small-scale versions of 'Tyneside flats', each containing only three rooms and occupied by the poorer sections of the population. Outside, there were back yards with lavatories. Whole families lived in these cramped conditions. It was a bleak environment, but the sense of community was strong, the friendly spirit of the people shone through their hardships. As the observer in 1885 had indicated, the poor helped the poor.

Men at work in the forge at Jarrow, c.1910. Men were laid off when work was slack, which caused great hardship to their families.

The Hospital

Charles Palmer was married three times. His first wife, Jane, daughter of Ebenezer Robson, of Newcastle, bore him four sons. One, Charles Mark, died in infancy in 1848 and another, also named Charles, died in 1898 in his late 40s. The surviving sons were George Robson Palmer and Alfred Molyneux Palmer.

Jane died in 1865 and Charles decided to pay for the building of an accident hospital in Jarrow as a memorial to her. Intended for the use of the company's workmen and their families, the Palmer Memorial Hospital opened in December 1870. Its running costs were met from the workmen's contributions with an annual grant from Palmers. The hospital was managed by a committee of officials from the yard and workmen's representatives. Its staff included a resident doctor, matron and nurses.

There could be no doubt that such a hospital was needed. Before it was built, men and boys injured in the shipyard or iron and steel works had to be taken by horse and cart to the Newcastle Infirmary. Some did not survive the journey. Jane had expressed sympathy and concern for these unfortunate workers and it was therefore felt the hospital would be an appropriate memorial to her.

Accidents at Palmers were an all too common occurrence. Indeed, it is said that at least one accident happened every week. Some were serious and death was often the result. Hard helmets, hand rails, guard rails and safety nets were unheard of in those days. Men worked on the open-air shipbuilding berths in conditions which today would be regarded as extremely dangerous.

The iron and steel works too had its share of casualties. For example, in November 1896 it was reported that George Kirsopp, a boy aged 14, had been killed at the works when he became entangled in a machine. In March of that year Henry Campbell, aged 38, of Walter Street, was killed at the works when he was struck by a locomotive while crossing one of the company railway lines.

An example of another railway tragedy occurred in February 1905 when John Baird, of Oak Street, a widower with seven children, was killed at the Palmers railway crossing in Western Road. This was a point at which lines entered the works from outside and was clearly a dangerous area for pedestrians. The unfortunate John Baird was said to have been deaf through being a riveter in the shipyards and because of this he did not hear the train. A fund was started to help his orphan children.

Charles Palmer with his first wife, Jane. The Palmer Memorial Hospital was built as a tribute to Jane following her death in 1865.

Even after the First World War fatal accidents were by no means uncommon. In early 1922, for example, William Anderson, a rigger, fell from a ship under construction at the Jarrow yard. He was taken to the Palmer Memorial Hospital but died on arrival. His wife, Esther, who ran a shop, was left a widow with a large family.

William was from Sligo, one of the many Irishmen who came to Jarrow to find work in the yard. Over the years, a large Irish community therefore developed in the town and made an important contribution to its social and cultural life. In addition, there was an also an influx of Scots, who likewise made their valuable contribution to the town's life.

In the late 1880s an extension to the Memorial Hospital, known as the 'Jubilee Wing', was opened. A ward in this extension became a 'lying-in' (maternity) facility for the wives of workmen who contributed to the hospital's upkeep. However, by this time many of the medical facilities had been extended to the other residents of the town.

Jane Palmer had carried out many acts of kindness for the workmen and a stained glass window was put in place at the hospital as a tribute to her. The inscription read: 'In memory of Jane, the beloved wife of C.M. Palmer, Esq., of Whitley Park, who died April 6, 1865, aged 43 years. Erected in grateful memory of her many acts of kindness by the workmen of Palmer Bros. & Co., and friends.'

Exactly 50 years after the hospital was founded, a new outpatients' department was opened by Sir Alfred Molyneux Palmer, in December 1920. Following the collapse of the company in 1933 the hospital was run by the town council and in 1948 it was taken over by the newly-created National Health Service.

After the Second World War, minor casualties were still treated at the hospital and consultants from Newcastle regularly visited. Minor operations were also carried out and there was a dermatology unit and outpatient clinics. By the 1960s the hospital had 29

The Palmer Memorial Hospital which opened in December 1870. Before it was built, men and boys in the shipyard or iron and steel works had to be taken by horse and cart to the Newcastle Infirmary.

beds, which consisted of 17 post surgical and 12 dermatology. 'Walk-in' casualties were still catered for, although ambulance cases went to South Shields.

In November 1983 the hospital was closed and later demolished. A new one, the Palmer Community Hospital, was completed nearby in 1986. The memorial stained glass window was removed from the old building and installed in the staircase area of the new hospital, a permanent reminder of Jane Palmer, a lady who had clearly impressed the workmen of Jarrow.

A Palmer Quartet

almers built more than 100 warships for the Royal Navy, but the output of the slipways was nevertheless dominated by merchant vessels. As well as steam colliers, the ships launched included cargo liners, tramp steamers, oil tankers and sailing vessels.

Tiny ferries were also built for cross-Tyne duties between Jarrow and Howdon. In contrast, from 1857 to 1873 the company turned out ocean-going passenger ships for the Guion, National and North German Lloyd lines.

The output for North German Lloyd included the *Mowe*, *Adler*, *Schwan* and *Schwalbe*. These 'little' ships were each just over 500 gross tons, but despite their modest dimensions served on the transatlantic run between Bremen and New York. They were followed by the more substantial *Hudson* and *Weser*, constructed for the same company, which were both 2,250 gross tons. All were built between 1856 and 1859.

The Guion Line received considerably larger ocean queens, many ranging from 3,100 to 4,300 gross tons, in the 1860s and early 1870s. They were also designed for transatlantic service. The largest were the *Montana* and *Dakota*, launched, unusually, with their engines and boilers aboard. Of smaller size were the *Manhattan*, *Chicago*, *Minnesota*, *Colorado*, *Nevada*, *Idaho*, *Wyoming* and *Wisconsin*.

Manhattan was the first Guion Line ship and opened the company's Liverpool-New York service in 1866. She was 343ft long with a gross tonnage of 2,866. The vessel could carry 72 first-class passengers and 800 in second class. She could also take aboard 1,500 tons of cargo. Comfort and ventilation in the second class accommodation received particular praise for being well above the average standard for the early steamship era.

One of these ships, the *Chicago*, was wrecked when she struck rocks while shrouded in fog near the entrance to Cork harbour. However, all the 130 passengers and crew were landed safely in the ship's lifeboats within a short space of time.

Vessels built for the National Line included the *Ontario*, *Helvetia*, *England*, *Scotland* and *Ireland*, all of similar size to the Guion steamers. They left the Palmers slipways in the 1860s.

Also from Palmers were the two-funnel Royal Mail paddle steamers *Connaught* and *Hibernia*, built to run between Western

The handsome Royal Mail paddle steamer Connaught, *built for the Galway Line, launched at Jarrow in 1860.*

Ireland and North America. Constructed for the Galway Line, the *Connaught* was launched at Jarrow on April 11 1860 by Charles's first wife, Jane. She was a large ship for her day with a length of 360ft and a gross tonnage of 2,959. Her paddle wheels were an impressive 34ft in diameter.

The *Connaught* was certainly a beautiful vessel, but her life was to prove all too brief. On July 11, 1860, she sailed on her maiden voyage from Galway to St Johns in Newfoundland, Canada, and then on to Boston in the USA. The passage took eight days.

It seemed a favourable start to a useful career. However, her second voyage was to end in disaster. On September 25 1860 the ship left St Johns bound for Boston with 591 passengers and crew aboard under the command of a Captain Leitch. After two days she began taking in water and a list to port developed. The crew tried to correct this, but she then began listing to starboard. Despite the problem they renewed their efforts and eventually managed to get her on to an even keel.

Everyone on board must have breathed sighs of relief. Then, on October 7, one of the funnels overheated and this set lagging alight. The flames spread. Soon much of the ship was ablaze and there was no choice but to abandon her. However, there was no loss of life as the passengers and crew were all rescued by the American brigantine *Minnie Schiffer*. The hapless *Connaught* was now on fire from stem to stern. It was a sad fate for such a handsome paddle steamer which had been in service barely three months.

The *Hibernia*, also ordered by the Galway Line, was launched on September 1 1860. She does not seem to have served more than eight years on the North Atlantic route, being sold in c.1869 to the City of Dublin Steam Packet Company and renamed *Leinster*. It is likely she served for some time as an Irish Sea ferry. The *Leinster*'s career ended in 1877 when she was wrecked off the coast of Brazil, near Sao Luiz.

The year 1866 saw Palmers launch the *Jumna*, a ship designed to carry British troops to India. Capable of embarking around 1,000 soldiers, she had a crew of 300. The *Jumna* was said to have used her sails frequently to conserve fuel. She lasted for many years.

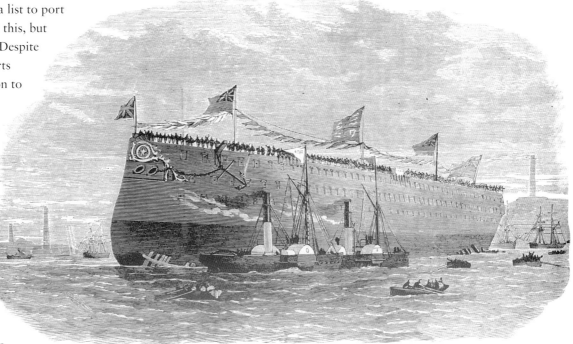

Launch of the troopship Jumna *in September 1866. She was built to carry soldiers from Britain to India.*

25

An observer described her launch in September 1866: 'This afternoon the magnificent troopship *Jumna*, built for Her Majesty's government, was launched from Messrs. Palmers' Shipyard in the presence of a large number of invited people and in sight also of a much more numerous assemblage of uninvited spectators.

'The ship was for a period of nearly two years in building on the stocks and her immense length was fully seen as she lay athwart the river. The state of the weather sadly marred the enjoyment of the launch as the rain fell in torrents and wetting all concerned in the launch, especially the guard of honour and the bandsmen of the 1st Durham Engineers.'

What seems to have been the same observer described her departure from the river in June the following year: 'The troopship *Jumna* left the Tyne this morning about 7am. Having left her moorings she hoisted the White Ensign and pendant and proceeded down the river in the tow of the tug steamers *Robert Scott*, *Fiery Cross*, *Stephensons* and *Tyne*.

'Steam was up but was not put into operation until at the entrance to the Narrows when the screw was set in motion and worked admirably. After getting to sea, she went on a trial over the measured mile at Whitley Bay. She afterwards proceeded to Plymouth in charge of a North Sea pilot named Mr Hindhaugh who remained on board until the end of the voyage.'

Passenger ships and a large troopship naturally attracted a great deal of attention, but more mundane vessels proved to be the most important source of business. Oil tankers, for example, featured prominently in the list of Palmer orders. More than 90 tankers made their way down the company's slipways.

Between 1872 and 1874 the firm built three combined oil tank-passenger ships, the *Vaderland*, *Nederland* and *Switzerland* for the Antwerp-based company Red Star Line, but there is no proof they ever carried oil. It may be that the cargo was considered too dangerous. They had been intended to carry passengers from Europe to America and bring oil back on the return voyage.

Palmers also produced steam yachts such as Vagrant, *pictured here. The* Vagrant *was launched in 1903 for Charles P. Markham, a director of Palmers. The elegant vessel survived the Second World War.*

The first true oil tanker from Palmers was the *Era*, launched on January 22 1887 by Miss Mary Price, a daughter of the company's general manager, John Price. Rigged as a three-masted schooner, the steel-hulled *Era* was 271ft long and equipped with triple expansion engines built by the firm.

A veritable fleet of these vessels then followed, with oil businesses flocking to Palmers, especially between 1912 and 1917. The 1920s also saw a whole series of tankers constructed for several firms, including the British Tanker Company, Venezuela Gulf Oil and Eagle Oil. Indeed, the order book of the 1920s was dominated by tankers. The largest of these were the *San Gaspar*, launched in 1921, and *San Gerardo*, launched the following year, both for Eagle Oil and each of just under 13,000 deadweight tonnes.

In addition to tankers, cargo liners were another mainstay of the business, with numerous launchings for such well known companies as the Hamburg America, Ellerman and Elder, Dempster lines.

More romantic vessels also took shape on the building berths such as the steam yachts *Vagrant* and *Cornelia*. The elegant *Cornelia*, for example, was built by Palmers for County Durham coal owner the Marquis of Londonderry. This beautiful vessel was 200ft long with a beam of 25ft and was rigged as a three-masted schooner. She was equipped with 120 hp engines, said to be 'highly finished'. The yacht was named after the marquis's wife and completed in 1880.

The oil tanker Rotterdam, *launched by Palmers in January 1895 for the American Petroleum Company of Rotterdam. She was launched by Mrs Voege, wife of the marine superintendent of the oil company. The ship was just one of the many oil tankers built by Palmers.*

Twelve years previously the marquis had received a similar pleasure steamer from the company, also named *Cornelia* but of smaller size. The design of the new steam yacht was reported to have been left entirely to Palmers because of the marquis's confidence in the firm.

On May 20 1880, the second *Cornelia* left the Tyne on her trial trip to sea. She achieved 13 knots on the measured mile off Whitley Bay. A trial run was also made southwards along the County Durham coast to the Tees. During the trip a party of guests were given lunch on board, presided over by general manager John Price.

But whether they were built for pleasure, trade or defence, the birth of ships always attracted attention on the banks of the Tyne. Launches were proud moments for the workmen as they saw the results of their labours afloat at last.

Charles Palmer seems to have been more than aware of the publicity value of these occasions. On August 15 1863 he arranged the simultaneous launch of four ships, a feat which must have drawn large crowds. Two vessels, the *Europa* and *Latona*, entered the Tyne from the Jarrow yard and two others, the *John McIntyre* and the *No. 1*, from the Howdon yard, a little way upstream on the opposite bank. It was a masterpiece of co-ordination.

A gun was fired as the signal for the four ships to slide down the ways at the same time. The 'Palmer quartet' took to the water without mishap. The gun was then fired a second time to mark the successful completion of this extraordinary Tyneside event. The quartet were now sisters of the Tyne, proudly riding on its waters and sharing the same birthday.

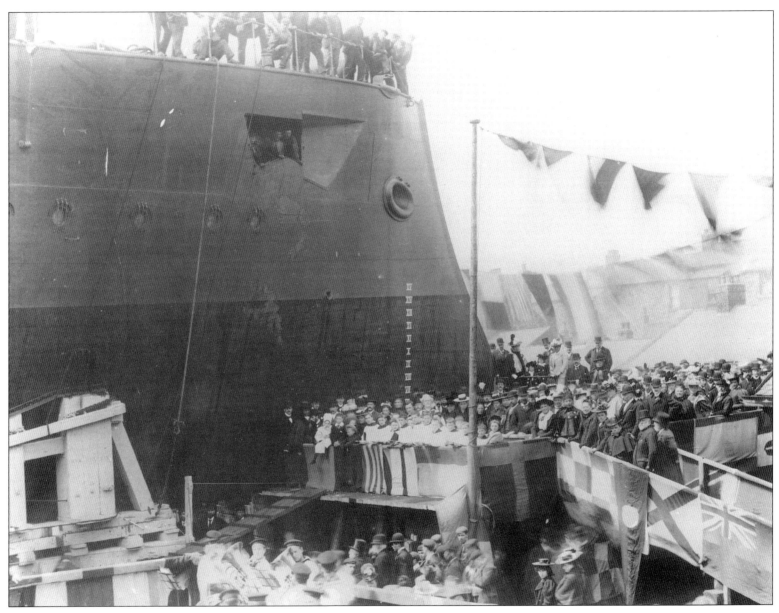

A launch day at Jarrow. Workmen stand on the bow of the ship and also peer through the anchor aperture. These were occasions when the more comfortably off members of society and working men and their families came face to face.

Mayor and Baronet

In 1862 Charles Palmer's brother, George, retired from the company. During 1865, the same year in which his first wife died, Charles transformed his business, Palmer Brothers & Company, into a limited liability company under the name Palmers Shipbuilding & Iron Company Ltd.

Charles married for a second time two years later, in 1867. This time his bride was Augusta Mary, daughter of Alfred Lambert, of Paris. Augusta bore him two sons, Claud Bowes Palmer and Lionel Hugo Palmer. Following her death, he married Gertrude, daughter of James Montgomery, of Cranford, in 1877. The children from this marriage were Godfrey Mark Palmer and Hilda Palmer. Charles thus had seven sons and a daughter from his three marriages.

But the highly successful entrepreneur was not content to remain only a businessman. For more than 30 years he served as an MP in the House of Commons. His first foray into politics was in 1868 when he fought for the South Shields parliamentary seat but was defeated. However, in 1874 he was elected Liberal member for the North Durham constituency and continued to hold this seat until 1885 when, on the reorganisation of seats, he was elected as the member for Jarrow. He was to retain this seat until his death in 1907.

In 1875 Jarrow achieved borough status, receiving a charter of incorporation in June that year. The first borough elections took place two months later, with Charles Palmer topping the poll in South Ward. Afterwards, he was elected the first mayor of the borough at the council's inaugural meeting. However, Charles did not remain mayor for long. He retired after only three months, but pre-

Charles Palmer with his second wife, Augusta Mary. They married in 1867.

sented the borough with a gold chain for his successor.

His decision not to serve for a full year was almost certainly due to his business and parliamentary commitments. Indeed, Charles was a man of many parts. He was, for a time, a director of the Suez Canal Company, a deputy lieutenant of County Durham and the North Riding of Yorkshire and twice president of Newcastle and Gateshead Chamber of Commerce. He also served as honorary colonel of the Newcastle and Durham Engineer Volunteers.

In 1864 the Jarrow Mechanics'

The unveiling of the statue of Sir Charles Palmer in front of the Memorial Hospital on 30 January 1904. The ceremony was performed by Lady Gertrude Palmer, Charles' third wife. Sir Charles was present to witness the event.

Institute was opened and provided with a library containing over 6,000 books, reading and billiard rooms and a large public hall. Charles had helped in its foundation, the company providing finance for the building. The Mechanics' Institute was designed to give working men the opportunity to better themselves through education, but it is difficult to believe many workers had the energy or enthusiasm to study after long, tiring hours of arduous labour in the shipyard or iron and steel works.

The year 1886 was another milestone in the career of a man who could be called 'Mr Jarrow'. He was created a baronet in recognition of his public services, becoming Sir Charles rather than 'Mr'.

More honours followed for this shipbuilding luminary. He was host to the Prince of Naples (later King of Italy) who visited the Jarrow yard in 1891 and entertained the prince at his Jesmond home. Less than a year later Sir Charles was made a Commander of the Order of St Maurice and Lazarus of Italy. Lazarus was the patron saint of the Knights Hospitallers, and it is likely he received the honour for providing the hospital at Jarrow.

However, the year 1893 marked a low-point in Sir Charles's career. He resigned as chairman of the company after the business suffered a period of financial losses. But this did not diminish his standing in the community.

A sign of the high esteem in which he was still held came in 1902-03, when, at the age of 80, Sir Charles was Mayor of Jarrow for a second time. Soon afterwards, in 1904, he achieved what he may have regarded as his greatest honour. Some of the older employees of Palmers had set up a fund to erect a statue of the industrial baronet to commemorate his life's work. Friends also subscribed to the scheme.

The statue, by sculptor Albert Toft, was sited in front of the memorial hospital and was unveiled by Lady Gertrude Palmer on January 30, 1904. Sir Charles was there to witness the event and it was believed to have given him great pleasure. It is unusual for a statue to be dedicated to a still living man.

The *Palmers Record*, an occasional journal published by the company, commented after his death: 'Sir Charles was indeed always popular with the workmen. They recognised the part he had played in the industrial life of the North, and the monument they erected will serve to remind posterity not only of the esteem in

Sir Charles Palmer aged 82, two years before his death.

which they held the founder of the company, but also the chivalrous and manly character of those who put it there. In honouring their late employer they honoured themselves.'

It is evident that Sir Charles had a loyal following amongst a considerable number of Jarrow's people. A decisive number of the town's electors voted for him at general elections, ensuring his continuing membership of Parliament. Although he stood as a Liberal, the Conservatives did not contest his Jarrow seat, apparently recognising the solid support enjoyed by the great industrialist.

Various Labour candidates opposed Sir Charles at the elections in 1885, 1902 and 1906 but were unable to wrest the seat from him. However, at a by-election a month after his death in 1907 Pete Curran was elected as Independent Labour MP for the constituency. Ironically, the baronet had planned to retire from politics that year.

It seems that Sir Charles had what might be called a 'personal' following in Jarrow. It was probably the awe and respect in which he was held as the founder of the shipyard and leading light of the town which had kept his vote buoyant for so many years.

The baronet had homes in Jesmond, Newcastle, in Mayfair, London, and at Grinkle Park, a country estate in North Yorkshire, not far from the company's iron ore mines at Hinderwell, close to Port Mulgrave. He lived the life of a typical Victorian industrialist and man of wealth. By contrast, and again typical of the Victorian era, most of his workmen and their families endured a low standard of living, which descended into poverty in times of unemployment.

Sir Charles died on June 4, 1907, at his home in Curzon Street, Mayfair, aged 84. He was buried at Easington Parish Church, North Yorkshire, near his Grinkle Park home and Port Mulgrave. It is curious that the man most associated with the great shipbuilding town of Jarrow should not have been laid to rest there.

This did not, of course, stop the community from paying its respects to the honoured businessman and politician. The Jarrow yard was shut down for the day of his funeral. Playing the *Dead*

March, the Palmer works band led a large procession of workmen from the yard gates shortly before 2pm. They walked to Jarrow's 'Old Church' for a memorial service. A similar service was held at the town's Christ Church.

The *Palmers Record* declared that Sir Charles 'took a warm and almost paternal interest' in the town of Jarrow until the end of his life. Small wonder that men dubbed it 'Palmerstown.'

Palmer's monument around 1920. Older men sit below the monument, now blackened by Jarrow smoke. Many years later the statue was removed to the riverside at Jarrow.

Tyne landmark. The cableway cranes at the Jarrow shipyard, the first of which were installed in 1906 (see page 35). They were a distinctive feature of the river until they were demolished around 1934-35 after the collapse of the company.

The Splendid Cat

In 1911 Palmers leased the former Robert Stephenson shipyard at Hebburn, which contained nine building berths and the largest dry dock on the East Coast. The following year the company purchased the yard, which also featured a large steel gantry fitted with an electric travelling crane running along rails.

The 700ft-long Hebburn dry dock was to prove a wonderful asset to the company. It enabled Palmers to undertake repair work to larger vessels than those handled at Jarrow.

As well as repairs, ships were built at the Hebburn site until the closure of Palmers in 1933. The yard launched 91 vessels for the company, the first being the cargo liner *City of Birmingham* which slid down the ways in August 1911. These were followed shortly afterwards by the refrigerated cargo liners *La Negra* and *La Rosarina*, constructed for the British and Argentine Steam Navigation Company. Also in 1911, the yard produced two dock gates for India.

The purchase of Hebburn in 1912 coincided with the sale of the company's Howdon yard to J.T. Eltringham Ltd. Numerous colliers had been constructed on the Howdon berths, but the last

Mighty warship. The battlecruiser HMS Queen Mary *is launched into the Tyne from the Jarrow shipyard on 20 March 1912, the ceremony being performed by Viscountess Allendale. The vessel was Palmers' largest warship.*

Palmer vessels from this yard were two warships, the cruiser HMS *Pyramus* and the torpedo-boat destroyer HMS *Flirt,* both launched in 1897.

In 1906, the first of two electric cableway crane networks was installed at Jarrow. The second network was erected in c.1912. These distinctive structures made the shipyard instantly recognisable and became something of a landmark on the river.

They featured huge lattice-work towers supporting elliptical-shaped gantries. Attached to the gantries were a series of cableways running above the building berths. Trolley cranes ran along these cableways to service the ships under construction. These structures were unique to Britain, the only other shipyard featuring such installations being at Bilbao in Spain.

Crowds watch the Queen Mary *leave Jarrow on 30 August 1913.*

Soon the aerial trolley cranes were busy working on a prestigious vessel of mighty proportions. In May 1909 it was announced that the company had won the order to build the prestigious battlecruiser HMS *Queen Mary*. She was to be the largest warship ever constructed by Palmers and it was reported that within hours of the news carpenters had begun preparing the berth at Jarrow.

HMS *Queen Mary*'s keel was laid down on March 6 1911. She was to be a Lion Class battlecruiser, warships of this type being nicknamed the 'Splendid Cats'. Indeed, this description summed up their essential qualities – they were long, powerful, sleek and fast.

Battlecruisers were designed to have great fire power but were not as heavily armoured as their close relatives, the battleships. This relatively lighter armour enabled them to attain greater speed.

Displacing around 27,000 tons, the *Queen Mary*'s turbine engines generated 75,000 hp, giving her a service speed of 27.5 knots. This was very fast at that time for such a large warship. The vessel was equipped with no less than 42 boilers. Her main armament consisted of eight 13.5-inch guns mounted in four massive turrets. She was 703ft long with a maximum beam of 89ft amidships. Her armour varied in thickness from nine inches to one inch.

Jarrow's impressive *Queen Mary* was launched into the Tyne on March 20 1912, the ceremony being performed by Viscountess Allendale. A huge crowd of spectators was admitted to the yard by special ticket and the main guests were accommodated on two platforms in front of the ship's bows. Hundreds of people also viewed the launch from vantage points on both sides of the Tyne, including the ballast hills at Willington Quay.

The *Newcastle Daily Journal* reported that 'the huge vessel moved slowly down the ways and entered her destined element with a graceful curtsey to the cheering multitude'. The band of the Durham Fortress Engineers (Territorials) played *A Life on the Ocean Wave*, followed by *Rule Britannia* and *God Save The King*.

There was a distance of only 70 or 80ft of water in which the huge ship could be turned by tugs after the launch to prevent her grounding on the opposite bank. As a precaution, the gangway at the Howdon ferry landing had been removed and a temporary landing was installed near Willington Quay police station.

Queen Mary, wife of King George V, sent the following message to Viscountess Allendale: 'I am so grateful to you for so kindly representing me at the launch of HM ship *Queen Mary* today, and I sincerely hope all prosperity will follow the ship which has been named after me.'

After the ceremony was finished the main guests were provided with refreshments in the mould loft, presided over by Lord Furness, who was chairman of Palmers at the time.

HMS *Queen Mary* was completed in August 1913, a year before the outbreak of the First World War. As she departed the Tyne on August 30 1913 on her way to be commissioned into the Royal Navy, no one could have foreseen that in less than three years Jarrow's 'Splendid Cat' would be sunk with great loss of life at the Battle of Jutland.

But Jutland was not to be her only clash with the enemy. HMS *Queen Mary* took part in the Battle of Heligoland Bight almost exactly a year after she left the Tyne. In this engagement she joined a force of British ships which attacked a patrol of German light cruisers and destroyers on August 28 1914. The *Queen Mary* sank two out of three enemy vessels lost in the fight. No British ships were lost, although one was badly damaged.

At first, the war must have seemed distant from the Tyne, but within a year of Heligoland Bight it was to reach the heart of Jarrow with fatal consequences. On the night of June 15, 1915, the Germans mounted a Zeppelin raid on Tyneside – the shipyards being a major target. Bombs rained down from a Zeppelin on to the Jarrow yard and 12 workers were killed when the fitting and coppersmiths workshops were hit. Among the dead was a young man aged 18. He was George Ward, of Church Street in the town, who had been working night shift. It was a poignant reminder that war could now kill civilians far from the battlefields.

The total number of people who lost their lives along the banks of the river in the airship raid was 16, including a police constable at Howdon. A 17th death was later linked to the raid. Isabella Laughlin, a widow aged 60, of Richard Street, Jarrow, was reported to have been awoken by the bombing at 11.40pm and to have seen the Zeppelin. She died shortly afterwards. At the inquest, a verdict was recorded of 'Death from syncope [another name for fainting] following shock caused by the visit of a hostile aircraft.' As well as the deaths, up to 40 people were reported wounded by the bombing. It was a traumatic episode for the people of Tyneside.

The air raid had taken place while the torpedo-boat destroyer HMS *Nonsuch* was under construction at Jarrow. The little ship does not seem to have been damaged and she was launched into the Tyne six months later on December 7, 1915. Displacing 1,200 tons, the *Nonsuch* was completed in February the following year, in time to join the British Grand Fleet at the Battle of Jutland three months later.

A squadron of battlecruisers in this immense clash of warships was under the command of Rear Admiral Sir David Beatty, who had also been commander at Heligoland Bight. It was in May 1916 that Beatty, flying his flag in HMS *Lion*, led his battlecruisers, including HMS *Queen Mary*, into the North Sea on a mission of great moment. His orders were to lure the German High Seas Fleet towards the British Grand Fleet with its colossal fire power.

Beatty's ships encountered a German battlecruiser squadron under Vice Admiral Franz von Hipper who, ironically, had been given orders to lure the British squadron into an ambush by his country's High Seas Fleet. But there was a key difference in the tac-

Tragic giant. The battlecruiser HMS Queen Mary at the mouth of the Tyne as she departs the river on her delivery voyage on 30 August 1913. In less than three years this impressive warship was sunk with great loss of life at the Battle of Jutland.

tics of the two sides. The Germans were only seeking to destroy Beatty's battlecruisers and did not wish to take on the entire British Grand Fleet which was numerically superior. Indeed, they did not know at this stage that the British fleet had put to sea.

The first phase of the Battle of Jutland began on the afternoon of May 31 as the British and German battlecruisers came into contact with one another on the eastern fringes of the North Sea, close to the entrance to the Skaggerak off Denmark's Jutland peninsula. The huge guns of these warships began roaring out from both sides.

Soon Beatty's flagship, *Lion*, had been badly hit and a fire raged in one of the turrets. It was a potentially disastrous situation, but the ship was saved by a fatally wounded Royal Marine officer who ordered the magazine below the turret to be flooded.

Other British ships were not to be so lucky. HMS *Indefatigable*, at the rear of Beatty's line, was hit by shells from the German battlecruiser *Von der Tann*. She was blown to pieces by a formidable explosion and sank with the loss of 1,010 officers and men. There were only two survivors.

Meanwhile, a fight had developed between the *Queen Mary* and the German battlecruisers *Seydlitz* and *Derfflinger*. The gunners of the *Queen Mary* had a reputation for being the crackshots of the fleet and they seemed to be living up to this reputation when they scored several hits on the German ships. Their shelling silenced a turret in *Seydlitz*.

However, the *Queen Mary* was then hit by devastating salvoes from the *Derfflinger* or *Seydlitz*. After being struck forward and then amidships by the shells she was torn apart by two explosions as her magazines blew up. Fierce fires broke out aboard the Tyne ship and she began listing steeply to port.

The second explosion blew chunks of steel, a picket boat and documents high into the air and the vessel began sinking. The metal debris rained down on passing British ships. A giant pall of black smoke towered hundreds of feet into the air above the shat-

tered *Queen Mary* as she went down. When the smoke began to clear, the stern of Jarrow's tragic battlecruiser could be seen projecting out of the water. So sudden had been her destruction that her propellers were still revolving. Then another blast sounded out from inside the ship and the Tyne's 'Splendid Cat' sank into the depths of the North Sea.

The *Queen Mary* went down with the loss of 1,266 officers and men, a terrible death toll by any standards. There were only nine survivors. Seven crew were rescued by a British destroyer and two by a German ship. Among the long list of the dead was Sub-Lieutenant the Hon. Algernon W. Percy, of the Royal Naval Reserve, a grandson of the 6th Duke of Northumberland and nephew of the 7th Duke.

In sharp contrast to the *Queen Mary*, the torpedo-boat destroyer HMS *Nonsuch* survived Jutland. She was attached to the 12th Destroyer Flotilla during the battle. The small Jarrow vessel lived on until after the war and did not go to the breaker's yard until May 1921. The battleship HMS *Hercules*, launched by Palmers in 1910, was another Jutland survivor.

During the First World War Palmers launched 23 vessels for the Royal Navy and docked and repaired 347 ships. The launchings included the hulls of two submarines, which were afterwards fitted out by Armstrong Whitworth on the Tyne.

Also during the conflict, 1,543 men from the Jarrow and Hebburn yards served in the British armed forces. Of these, 183 lost their lives.

Catastrophe

Following the First World War Palmers built a series of oil tankers and other vessels, but the business was hit by serious financial problems which, combined with the effects of the Great Depression, were to bring about its fall. However, more than 80 vessels were launched during the 1920s at Jarrow and Hebburn. In addition, there were six engines-only contracts.

In 1919 a large hostel, complete with a canteen, was opened by the company halfway between the Jarrow and Hebburn yards following an increase in the numbers of workmen employed. Known as Simpson's Hostel, it provided lodgings for workers who were unable to find accommodation because of a housing shortage in the district.

Many workmen were certainly still needed as orders came in for ships over the next few years, although an expected post-war boom in activity lasted only a couple of years and included a large amount of repair work. The year 1925 was a low-point for both yards, with only two ships, the *Langleeford* and *British Chemist*, being launched.

One of the more specialised vessels built during this decade was the cableship *Faraday*, launched for Siemen Brothers & Co., of London. Designed to lay and repair telephone and telegraph cables, the *Faraday* entered the water at Jarrow in February 1923. During the Second World War she did a spell as a Royal Navy training ship based in the River Dart, Devon.

Her career ended in June 1941 when the vessel was bombed by a German aircraft as she steamed in convoy from Falmouth on

Jim Cuthbert

Simpson's Hostel in Black Road, Hebburn, photographed in 1998. The hostel was built in 1919 to accommodate Palmers workmen. It provided lodgings for men who were unable to find accommodation because of a housing shortage in the district. A similar hostel was opened at Wallsend.

course for Milford Haven. The *Faraday* sank three miles north of St Anne's Head, South Wales. The ship's crew managed to shoot down the attacking plane, a Heinkel, but the stokehold and oil bunker had been hit by the bombs and she was engulfed by flames. Eight crewmen lost their lives and 25 were wounded.

Another important order in the 1920s was the cruiser HMS *York*, launched appropriately by the Duchess of York (later the Queen Mother) in 1928. Four other warships, all destroyers, were built by the company over the next few years. Those years were to be the final ones for Palmers.

The Depression of the early 1930s proved to be the death blow for the company. The worldwide slump led to the final closure of its steel works in 1931 with large numbers of men being thrown out of work. In any case, the steel works had been in decline for a decade and it suffered temporary closure for long periods in the 1920s. Now, with the Depression hitting business hard, shipbuilding too was in serious trouble.

The last merchant vessel to be constructed at the Jarrow yard was the tanker *Appalachee*, launched in October 1930 for the Anglo-American Oil Company. However, Palmers' last merchant ship, the tanker *British Strength*, was built at Hebburn. She was launched in February 1931 for the British Tanker Company and was the only vessel launched by the company that year. Times were now lean and the numbers employed at the yards were being run down.

The final ship from Palmers, the destroyer HMS *Duchess*, entered the water at Jarrow on July 19, 1932. She was the 982nd vessel built by the company. There was no ceremony or major publicity. The Depression was gripping Britain and unemployment had already grown rapidly in the town. There were no more orders and thousands of men in the district were on the dole.

Palmers had already become financially weak and with the onset of the slump was unable to weather the economic storm. In 1931 the company had recorded losses totalling £119,000 and it lacked the reserves to survive.

By the beginning of 1933, more than 7,000 people were unemployed in Jarrow, around 70 per cent of the town's workforce. The company was now heavily in debt and creditors were clamouring for payment. A possibility of an order from the Royal Navy came to nothing.

At the end of June 1933 a receiver was drafted in to take over the affairs of the collapsed business. The following year the receiver sold Palmers to National Shipbuilders Security Ltd., a firm which had been set up by other shipbuilding companies to reduce overcapacity in the industry by acquiring and closing down yards. Its actions were to stir up much controversy.

National Shipbuilders Security Ltd then sold the Jarrow yard to a demolition firm. By 1935 this firm had moved in to dismantle most of the yard. Its equipment was sold off. Within a few years, the distinctive elliptical-shaped gantries of the cableway crane network had disappeared into history. By a covenant of the sale, no more shipbuilding was to be allowed on the site for 40 years.

The social consequences of these moves were catastrophic for the people of the town and surrounding area. The community's dependency on the shipyard was so great that Jarrow was engulfed by mass unemployment. Few families remained untouched by this unprecedented social and economic disaster. Adding to their woes, unemployment benefit had been reduced by the National Government. A scheme by businessman T. Vosper Salt to build a new, modern steel works on the yard site collapsed after opposition from rival steel businesses.

To qualify for unemployment benefit, and when that ran out, for Public Assistance, men had to prove they were spending almost every waking hour actively looking for work.

The most hated measure introduced by the government was the means test. This involved an examination in detail of a family's possessions and financial circumstances, including any hard-earned savings.

A ship is born. The launch of the cruiser HMS York at Jarrow in 1928. The ceremony was performed by the Duchess of York, later the Queen Mother.

Under the means test, bailiffs would go to an unemployed man's home and household possessions, except the bare necessities of life, were valued and ordered to be sold. The family would then be told how many weeks the proceeds would have to last them before they could re-apply for Public Assistance relief. Grown-up children in work often left home because even if their earnings were low their family's relief payments would be reduced or stopped if they remained under the same roof.

Agencies set up offices in the town seeking to enroll young women for employment in domestic service in London and other parts of the South. Young men in their hundreds left, either to join the armed forces, or to find jobs in the South. It was said that many a Jarrow lad met his future wife in Hyde Park, London, where a large contingent of them met every Sunday afternoon.

For the poorest of those left behind their diet consisted mainly of potatoes, broth, bread and jam, or simply bread and dripping. Women tried to make money by taking in washing, or by selling pies and peas or ginger beer from their homes. Men recovered driftwood from the river and attempted to sell it as firewood around the streets.

The famed Jarrow Crusade of October 1936 was a peaceful march which threw the spotlight on the poverty-stricken community and the unacceptable social effects of the Depression. Two hundred jobless men of the town marched over 280 miles from Jarrow to London in just under four weeks.

Each man was provided with a waterproof groundsheet which could be used as a cape in wet weather and a mouth organ band helped to keep their morale high as they paced southwards towards the capital. Jarrow Labour MP Ellen Wilkinson steadfastly championed their cause and accompanied the men along much of the route.

People in towns and cities they passed through backed their call for work and provided the men with food and accommodation. In Leeds, for example, they were treated to a splendid meal, and at

Jarrow MP Ellen Wilkinson leads the marchers into London in 1936.

Barnsley there was a particularly warm welcome which included a cooked meal and drinks. At Nottingham they were given clothing and boots as well as food and beds for the night, and when they reached Leicester cobblers mended their boots. It was a heartening display of sympathy and support.

Crusaders in capes. The Jarrow marchers enter London in a steady downpour, 1936, after walking nearly 300 miles.

The tired marchers reached central London in pouring rain. Headed by Ellen Wilkinson, they presented a petition to the House of Commons calling for work for the town's people.

However, wealthy philanthropist and businessman Sir John Jarvis, High Sheriff of Surrey and an MP, had felt a strong sympathy for the people of Jarrow and had already been instrumental in starting shipbreaking on the town's riverside in 1934 to provide the unemployed with temporary work. Under his leadership Surrey people subscribed to a fund for other projects to help the men and their families.

He now proposed to establish a new business, a metal tube works, in the town. In addition, he founded Jarrow Metal Industries, a concern which manufactured steel and alloy light castings. These schemes became a reality less than two years after the march, both works opening in May 1938.

The busy Jarrow ferry landing around 1930.

Another important development came in 1939 when a steel rolling mill was started by the Consett Iron Company on part of the former Palmer site, which had eventually been purchased by the Government. This gave a further welcome boost to jobs.

Sir John's efforts to provide work for the unemployed men included bringing the great passenger liners *Olympic*, sister ship of the *Titanic*, and *Berengaria* to the former yard for breaking up. Other vessels were also scrapped at the quay, including destroyers. In 1936 a Greek steamer was broken up. Some of the metal from the ships was supplied to the tube works and castings factory. The Surrey aid fund provided £2,000 towards dredging of the river alongside Palmers.

Olympic came to the Tyne on her final voyage in 1935 and *Berengaria* in 1938. They were among the largest vessels ever to enter the river. The lower hull of *Berengaria* was not taken to the

Firth of Forth for final scrapping until after the Second World War. One of the wooden deck houses from the *Olympic* was for many years used as offices at the Tyne Improvement Commission's Howdon yard.

Sir John Jarvis also set up a furniture-making works on part of the yard site and this provided more work. In addition, the unemployed were given the job of laying out a new recreational area in the borough – Monkton Dene Park – and wallpaper and paint were supplied for Jarrow people to redecorate their homes. These two projects were generously supported by the people of Surrey through the aid fund.

The praiseworthy industrial schemes did indeed reduce unemployment, but the new businesses did not employ as many people as the now lost shipyard and steel works. It was rearmament and the Second World War which finally sent the jobless figures plummeting, with men being needed at other shipyards and factories on the Tyne and, of course, for the armed forces.

A shipbuilding yard was never again opened in the town, but the Palmer facility at Hebburn continued to operate under the name of Palmers Hebburn Ltd. This company concentrated on ship repair and was owned by Vickers Armstrongs. Its dry dock at Hebburn was used to repair warships during the Second World War and continued in use for many years after the end of hostilities. The period of conflict from 1939 to 1945 saw Hebburn deal with 147 warships, including cruisers, and 291 merchant vessels. The dock lasted until the 1960s when it was filled in and a new one built

The smaller dry dock at Jarrow was likewise used for repair of ships during the war, although its operation was blocked until 1941 because the hulk of the *Berengaria* was lying across the dock entrance. However, in April that year the hulk was moved up river to a new berth

Palmers Shipyard at Hebburn, c.1912. Following the collapse of Palmers, National Shipbuilders Security Ltd. sold the Hebburn site to Vickers Armstrongs. Vickers operated the yard as a ship repair facility under the name Palmers Hebburn Ltd. The yard was used to repair ships during World War II. In later years it had several owners including Swan Hunter, Cammell Laird and, today, A & P Tyne.

and soon merchant ships and warships were being handled. The Jarrow dock, like its Hebburn counterpart, continued in use after the end of the conflict.

By the 1990s, the site of the Jarrow yard had become a small industrial estate. Among the firms now occupying this land is Rohm and Haas, the chemical company. A small fragment of the yard's eastern boundary wall still survives next to the trackway which led down to the Jarrow-Howdon ferry landing. It is close to

the entrance to the Tyne foot and cycle tunnel.

The lot of a Palmer workman was one of hard toil over long hours, a low standard of living, particularly for the unskilled, poverty during periods of unemployment caused by the uncertain and erratic nature of shipbuilding, and the constant danger of accidents which might seriously injure or kill. Added to this was the plight which a man's family would endure in times of unemployment, overcrowding, poor sanitation and the prevalence of infectious diseases which often led to the deaths of children as well as adults.

Despite all these hardships, the men of Jarrow, Howdon and Hebburn turned out fine ships of many types. Vessels crucial to economic success and to defence were born out of their unrelenting labour and their ordeals. Jarrow, the town shrouded in smoke, sent forth from its murky banks ships which contributed to the Tyne's renown as a river of skill and hard work.

In 1983 the statue of Sir Charles Palmer was transferred from its position in front of the memorial hospital to a small park on the riverside at Jarrow. Today, 'Sir Charles' gazes out across the Tyne, the great shipbuilding river which played such a leading role in his fortunes. Fittingly, he stands close to the spot where riveters' hammers once rang out from the yard over the constantly moving waters, creating ships to grace the world's oceans.

Contrasting worlds, above and facing. Saturday afternoon, 2 March, 1907, and a little vessel, Alpha, *is launched from the Jarrow yard by a group of children including Millicent Twadell, centre, youngest daughter of the shipyard manager. The boat, 51 feet long, was to be fitted with a Griffin oil engine and was experimental. She was intended for the company's use.*

Men pose for a picture in the boiler shop at the Hebburn yard c.1912. The yard launched 91 of the company's ships.

Chronology

1851-52 Charles Mark Palmer and his brother George set up a shipbuilding business at Jarrow.

1852 The Palmer shipyard's first vessel, the paddle tug *Northumberland*, is launched. Later the same year the pioneering iron steam collier *John Bowes* is launched.

1853 The Palmer steam collier *Jarrow* is the first ship to be provided with an engine built by the company.

1856 Palmers launches its first warship, the floating battery HMS *Terror*.

1857 Blast furnaces for the production of pig iron erected by the company.

1859 Palmers take over a shipyard at Howdon.

1862 The frigate HMS *Defence* completed.

1866 The troopship *Jumna* is launched.

1870 The Palmer Memorial Hospital opens in December.

1884 The company's first steel vessel, the *Albatross*, is launched.

1887 The first true oil tanker from Palmers, the *Era*, is launched.

1892 The first of the company's two battleships named HMS *Resolution* is launched.

1907 Sir Charles Palmer dies at the age of 84.

1911 Palmers take over the former Robert Stephenson yard at Hebburn.

1912 Launch of the battlecruiser HMS *Queen Mary*. Palmers sell the Howdon yard.

1915 Zeppelin raid on Tyneside. Twelve workers killed by bombing at the Jarrow yard.

1916 The battlecruiser HMS *Queen Mary* sunk at the Battle of Jutland on May 31 with the loss of 1,266 lives. Only nine survive.

1923 Launch of the cableship *Faraday*.

1928 Launch of the cruiser HMS *York*.

1930 The last of Palmers' merchant ships, the oil tanker *British Strength*, is launched at Hebburn.

1932 The company's final ship, the destroyer HMS *Duchess*, is launched at Jarrow. She is the 982nd vessel to be built by Palmers.

1933 HMS *Duchess* is completed. The company collapses and the Jarrow shipyard closes. The company goes into receivership. The town is gripped by mass unemployment.

1934 Receivers sell the Jarrow and Hebburn yards to National Shipbuilders Security Ltd. The Jarrow yard is later sold to a demolition firm. By a covenant of the sale, no more shipbuilding is to be allowed on the Jarrow site for 40 years. The Hebburn yard is sold to Vickers Armstrongs for shiprepair.

1935 The passenger liner *Olympic* is brought to Jarrow for breaking up. It provides temporary work for some of the unemployed men.

1936 The Jarrow Crusade. 200 unemployed men from Jarrow march to London to plead for work for the people of the town. Headed by the town's MP, Ellen Wilkinson, they present a petition to Parliament.

1938 A second passenger liner, the *Berengaria*, is brought to the town for breaking up. A tube works and metal castings factory are opened in Jarrow.

1939 A steel rolling mill is opened on part of the former Palmer yard site.

1939-45 The Hebburn yard repairs numerous warships and merchant vessels during the Second World War. From 1941 the old dry dock at the site of the Jarrow shipyard is also engaged in repair work.

Note: The Palmers' order list contains 1,007 yard numbers, but only 982 vessels were built. The remaining numbers were allotted to orders which were later cancelled, engines-only contracts and dock gates.